THE GRUFFALO'S CHILD
and other songs

Julia Donaldson

Illustrated by Axel Scheffler

MACMILLAN CHILDREN'S BOOKS

Introduction

by Julia Donaldson

Welcome to my third collection of songs for children. As in the first two books, *The Gruffalo Song and Other Songs* and *Room on the Broom and Other Songs*, the songs fall into two categories: story songs and action songs. So I hope they will appeal to primary schools, as well as children and parents at home, and that everyone will join in with the singing, actions and noises.

The story songs include "The Gruffalo's Child" and "Stick Man Song", which I wrote to go with those two books. "The World Inside a Book" was written to go with *Charlie Cook's Favourite Book*, though the idea is that the words can be adapted by children to fit their own favourite books. "The Mouse and the Lion" is a song version of the well-known Aesop's fable, and "Kitten on the Farm" is based on a French story.

Of the action songs, "I've Got a Ball of Pastry" is one I wrote when my second son was at nursery school. I used to go in and sing it with the children, who liked joining in and pretending to roll pastry, peel bananas and toss pancakes. "Nut Tree" is a more recent composition, which I often sing on stage, inviting audience members to curl up and then grow into trees (though there is usually one who fails to germinate!) "Breathing Song" provides an opportunity to gasp, pant, sniff, blow, and finally snore "so loud it wakes them up next door". "Swing and Spin" is an adaptation of the words of one of my "Songbirds" phonic reading books, but children too young to read can enjoy spinning, splashing and squelching. (This, by the way, is the Gruffalo's favourite song!)

As with the other two books, the songs have a simple piano accompaniment and guitar chords, but if no instrumentalist is on hand, the CD has instrument-only (karaoke) versions of all the songs as well as sung versions.

Once again, the marvellous arranger, Andrew Dodge, collected some great musicians to record the CD, on which I am also joined in song by my guitar-playing husband, Malcolm, and by Imogen Moore and her daughters, Lola and Amelie, plus the oboist's daughter, Rhiannon Morgan, who came to the studio with her mum and obligingly joined in the chorus of "Stick Man Song".

And, as usual, Axel Scheffler provided the icing on the cake with his lovely, humorous and colourful pictures, which I hope will inspire you all to sing and dance.

A note to accompanists, by the musical arranger, Andrew Dodge:

As the tunes and their accompaniments are scored across two staves, there is often only a single line in the right-hand part (the treble clef) so that the sung melody is as clear as possible. Consequently, there are often notes written in the left-hand part (the bass clef) that are more easily played with the right hand. Please play the bass clef notes with whichever hand is easier.

Contents

The Gruffalo's Child

With a Gruffalo lilt

1.Where are you go-ing to, Gruf-fa-lo's Child, all by your-self through the woods so wild? A-ha! O-
6.Where are you go-ing to, Gruf-fa-lo's Child, all by your-self through the woods so wild? A-way! Back

ho! To look for the Big Bad Mouse.
home! To hide from the Big Bad Mouse.

2.Where can he be? I'll ask the Snake. He's
3.Where can he be? Will Owl tell me? He's
4.Where can he be? The Fox looks sly: He's

*The lines in italics are sung
by the Gruffalo's Child;
the other lines are as follows:*

Verse 1: Narrator
Verse 2: Snake
Verse 3: Owl
Verse 4: Fox
Verse 5: Narrator

Verse 1
Where are you going to, Gruffalo's Child,
All by yourself through the woods so wild?
Aha! Oho!
To look for the Big Bad Mouse.

Verse 2
Where can he be? I'll ask the Snake.
He's down by the lake, eating Gruffalo cake.
Aha! Oho!
Beware of the Big Bad Mouse.

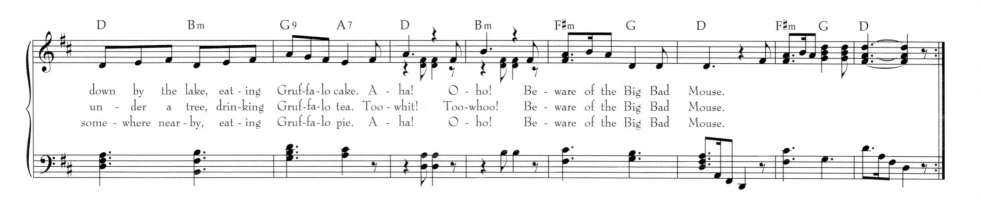

down by the lake, eat-ing Gruf-fa-lo cake. A - ha! O - ho! Be - ware of the Big Bad Mouse.
un - der a tree, drin-king Gruf-fa-lo tea. Too - whit! Too-whoo! Be - ware of the Big Bad Mouse.
some - where near-by, eat-ing Gruf-fa-lo pie. A - ha! O - ho! Be - ware of the Big Bad Mouse.

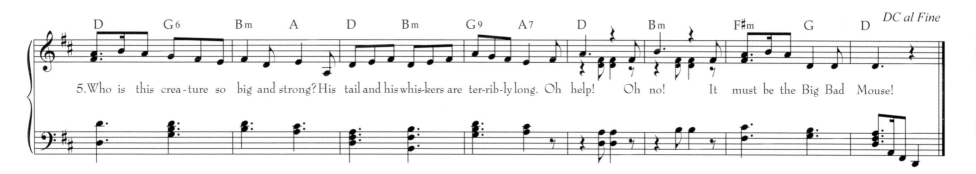

5. Who is this crea-ture so big and strong? His tail and his whis-kers are ter-rib-ly long. Oh help! Oh no! It must be the Big Bad Mouse!

Verse 3
Where can he be? Will Owl tell me?
He's under a tree, drinking Gruffalo tea.
Too-whit! Too-whoo!
Beware of the Big Bad Mouse.

Verse 4
Where can he be? The Fox looks sly:
He's somewhere nearby, eating Gruffalo pie.
Aha! Oho!
Beware of the Big Bad Mouse.

Verse 5
Who is this creature so big and strong?
His tail and his whiskers are terribly long.
Oh help! Oh no!
It must be the Big Bad Mouse!

Verse 6
Where are you going to, Gruffalo's Child,
All by yourself through the woods so wild?
Away! Back home!
To hide from the Big Bad Mouse.

I've Got a Ball of Pastry

Verse 1

I've got a ball of pastry.
What shall I do with that?

You've got to roll it, roll it, roll it,
Until you've rolled that pastry flat.
(Repeat)

Verse 4

I've got a jar of strawberry jam,
Sticky and sweet and red.

You've got to spread it, spread it, spread it,
Until it's on a slice of bread.
(Repeat)

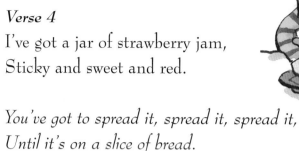

Verse 2

I've got a ripe banana.
Tell me where I begin.

You've got to peel it, peel it, peel it,
Until you've peeled off all the skin.
(Repeat)

Verse 5

I've got a flat, round pancake.
One side has just been fried.

You've got to toss it, toss it, toss it,
Until it lands the other side.
(Repeat)

Verse 3

I've got a pot of porridge,
Creamy and thick and hot.

You've got to stir it, stir it, stir it,
Until it's bubbling in the pot.
(Repeat)

Verse 6

I've got a plate of dinner.
What do you think that's for?

You've got to eat it, eat it, eat it,
And if it's nice you'll ask for more.
You've got to eat it, eat it, eat it,
And if it's nice you'll ask for more. MORE!

The Mouse and the Lion

Verse 1

In the hottest sun of the longest day,
A lion lay down for a doze.
A little brown mouse pattered out to play,
Pit-a-pat, pit-a-pat, he danced on
the whiskery nose.
Pit-a-pat, pit-a-pat, pit-a-pat, pit-a-pat,
He danced on the whiskery nose.

Verse 2

The lion awoke with a sneeze, "A-choo!"
He picked up the mouse in his paw.
"And who may I venture to ask are you?
Grrrrr!" he said with a terrible roar.
"*Grr, grrr, grrrrr, GRRRRRR!*"
He said with a terrible roar.

Verse 3

"I'll save your life if you'll let me go,"
The mouse's voice shook as he spoke.
The lion laughed loudly, "*Oho, oho,
ohohohoho!*
I'll let you go free for your joke.
Oho, oho, ohohohoho,
I'll let you go free for your joke."

6. For one of the les-sons which mice must learn from their whis-ke-ry fa-ther and mo-ther_____ is the fa-mous old say-ing that one good turn_____ al-ways de-serves a-no-ther.____ *Pit-a- pat. Grrr! O-ho-ho! Squeak!* Al-ways de-serves___ a - no-ther.____

slow down...............................

Verse 4

As chance would have it, the following week,
The lion was caught in a net.
When all of a sudden he heard a squeak:
"*Squeak, squeak,* well met, noble lion, well met.
Squeak, squeak, squeak, squeak,
Well met, noble lion, well met."

Verse 5

The little mouse nibbled and gnawed and bit
Till the lion was finally free.
"It's nothing, dear lion, don't mention it:
Nibbly, nibble, I'm repaying your kindness to me.
Nibbly, nibbly, nibbly, nibble,
Repaying your kindness to me."

Verse 6

For one of the lessons which mice must learn
From their whiskery father and mother
Is the famous old saying that one good turn
Always deserves another.
Pit-a-pat! Grrr! Ohoho! Squeak!
Always deserves another.

Stick Man Song

Delicately, like a stick man!

1.Stick Man lives in the fa-mi-ly tree___ with his Stick La-dy Love___ and their stick child-ren three.___ One

day he wakes ear-ly and goes for a jog. Stick Man, oh Stick Man, be - ware of the dog! Come back home, we're missing you, Stick Man! Come back

home to the fa-mi-ly tree. Come back home, we're miss-ing you, Stick Man! Come back home to the fa-mi-ly tree. 2."A
4.But

C   **E7**   **F**   **G7**   **C**   **E7**   **F**   **E7**   **Am**   **Em**

stick!" cries a girl with a smile on her face. "The right kind of pooh-stick for win-ning the race!" "A twig!" says a swan.___ "This
what is this chu-ckle that turns to a shout? "Oh - ho - ho - ho - ho, I'm STUCK! Get me OUT!" A stuck man? A stuck man? Now

F   _3_   **C**   **C#dim**   **Dm7**   **G7**   **C**   **Dm**   **G9**   **C**   **Am**

twig is the best! It's the right kind of twig to weave in-to my nest." Come back home, we're miss-ing you, Stick Man! Come back
who could that be? "Don't wor-ry!" says Stick Man, "I'll soon set you free."

F   **G7**   **C**   **C7**   **Dm**   **G9**   **C**   **Am**   **F**   **G7**   **C**   **C7**

home to the fa-mi-ly tree. Come back home, we're miss-ing you, Stick Man! Come back home to the fa-mi-ly tree. "A
Then

13

F   Em   Dm7   G9   C   C7   Dm   G7

mast!" cries a dad. "An ex-cel-lent mast! Hoo-ray! There's a flag on our cas-tle at last." "I'm not a mast for a

Stick Man helps San-ta de-li-ver the toys to fast-a-sleep girls and to fast-a-sleep boys. Fas-ter and fas-ter they

Em   A7   D   Dm7   G7   D   Dm6   G7

sil-ly old flag. Or a sword for a knight, or a hook for a bag."   3."An

fly through the snow, till__ San-ta says, "On-ly one chim-ney to go!"

1

C   E7   F   G7   C   E7   F   E7   Am   Em7   F   C

arm!" says a boy with a warm wool-ly scarf. "An arm for my snow-man," he says with a laugh. "A stick!" cries a mum. "A stick for the grate!"

Wake up, Stick Man, be - fore it's too late! Come back

slower

2. 5. Stick La-dy's lone - ly. The child-ren are sad. It won't feel like Christ - mas with-

Tempo 1

out their Stick Dad. But who is this tumb-ling in-to their house? Is it a bat, or a bird, or a mouse? Or could it be, or could it be

Stick Man, come back home to the fa-mi-ly tree? Yes it is! It really is Stick Man, stick-ing here in the fa-mi-ly tree!

slow down...........................

Verse 1

Stick Man lives in the family tree
With his Stick Lady Love and their stick children three.
One day he wakes early and goes for a jog.
Stick Man, oh Stick Man, beware of the dog!
Come back home, we're missing you, Stick Man!
Come back home to the family tree.
Come back home, we're missing you, Stick Man!
Come back home to the family tree.

Verse 2

"A stick!" cries a girl with a smile on her face.
"The right kind of pooh stick for winning the race!"
"A twig!" says a swan. "This twig is the best!
It's the right kind of twig to weave into my nest."
Come back home, we're missing you, Stick Man!
Come back home to the family tree.
Come back home, we're missing you, Stick Man!
Come back home to the family tree.

"A mast!" cries a dad. "An excellent mast!
Hooray! There's a flag on our castle at last."
"I'm not a mast for a silly old flag.
Or a sword for a knight, or a hook for a bag."

Verse 3

"An arm!" says a boy with a warm woolly scarf.
"An arm for my snowman," he says with a laugh.
"A stick!" cries a mum. "A stick for the grate!"
Wake up, Stick Man, before it's too late!
Come back home, we're missing you, Stick Man!
Come back home to the family tree.
Come back home, we're missing you, Stick Man!
Come back home to the family tree.

Verse 4

But what is this chuckle that turns to a shout?
"Oh, ho, ho, ho, ho – I'm STUCK! Get me OUT!"
A stuck man? A stuck man? Now who could that be?
"Don't worry!" says Stick Man, "I'll soon set you free."
Come back home, we're missing you, Stick Man!
Come back home to the family tree.
Come back home, we're missing you, Stick Man!
Come back home to the family tree.

Then Stick Man helps Santa deliver the toys
To fast asleep girls and to fast asleep boys.
Faster and faster they fly through the snow,
Till Santa says, "Only one chimney to go!"

Verse 5

Stick Lady's lonely. The children are sad.
It won't feel like Christmas without their Stick Dad.
But who is this tumbling into their house?
Is it a bat, or a bird, or a mouse?
Or could it be, or could it be Stick Man,
Come back home to the family tree?
Yes it is! It really is Stick Man,
Sticking here in the family tree!

Breathing Song

Starting lively, but sleepy by the end!

1.When you see a flower, do___ you sniff?
8.When you're fast a - sleep, do___ you snore?

When you see a flower, do___ you sniff?
When you're fast a - sleep, do___ you snore?

If it is a rose, a love - ly
Have you got a snore so loud it

Don't forget to make the sounds!

Verse 1

When you see a flower, do you sniff? *(Sniff)*
When you see a flower, do you sniff? *(Sniff)*
If it is a rose, a lovely smell goes up your nose,
When you sniff, *(Sniff)*
When you sniff. *(Sniff)*

Verse 2

When you climb a hill, do you pant? *(Pant)*
When you climb a hill, do you pant? *(Pant)*
When you're at the top, I bet you're really glad to stop,
And you pant, *(Pant)*
And you pant. *(Pant)*

Verse 3

When you get a shock, do you gasp? *(Gasp)*
When you get a shock, do you gasp? *(Gasp)*
Somebody says "Boo!" or there's a spider on your shoe,
So you gasp, *(Gasp)*
So you gasp. *(Gasp)*

Verse 4

When you have a cold, do you sneeze? *(A-choo)*
When you have a cold, do you sneeze? *(A-choo)*
Nothing you can do can stop it; here it comes – a-choo!
Yes, you sneeze, *(A-choo)*
Yes, you sneeze. *(A-choo)*

Verse 5

When your birthday comes, do you puff? *(Puff)*
When your birthday comes, do you puff? *(Puff)*
Maybe you can blow the candles out in just one go,
When you puff, *(Puff)*
When you puff. *(Puff)*

Verse 6

When you're feeling sad, do you sigh? *(Sigh)*
When you're feeling sad, do you sigh? *(Sigh)*
No one wants to play, and it's a cold and rainy day,
So you sigh, *(Sigh)*
So you sigh. *(Sigh)*

Verse 7

When you're feeling tired, do you yawn? *(Yawn)*
When you're feeling tired, do you yawn? *(Yawn)*
You grumbled when they said that it was nearly time for bed,
But you yawn, *(Yawn)*
Yes, you yawn. *(Yawn)*

Verse 8

When you're fast asleep, do you snore? *(Snore)*
When you're fast asleep, do you snore? *(Snore)*
Have you got a snore so loud it wakes them up next door,
When you snore, *(Snore)*
When you snore? *(Snore)*

Nut Tree

1. Small, brown, hard, round,
   The nut is lying underground.

4. And branches grow and stretch and spread,
   With twigs and leaves above your head.

2. Now a shoot begins to show.
   Now the shoot begins to grow.

5. And on a windy autumn day,
   The nut tree bends, the branches sway.

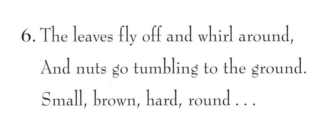

3. Tall, taller, tall as can be,
   The shoot is growing into a tree.

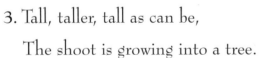

6. The leaves fly off and whirl around,
   And nuts go tumbling to the ground.
   Small, brown, hard, round . . .

Slow and majestic

Small, brown, hard, round, the nut is ly-ing un-der-ground. Now a shoot be-gins to show.

Now the shoot be-gins to grow. Tall, tal-ler, tall as can be, the shoot is grow-ing in-to a tree. And bran-ches grow and

stretch and spread, with twigs and leaves a-bove your head. And on a win-dy au-tumn day, the nut tree bends, the bran-ches sway. The

leaves fly off and whirl a-round and nuts go tum-bling to the ground. Small, brown, hard, round, the hard, round.

Repeat as required

Last time

Last time, slow down and repeat final 2 bars.

21

Kitten on the Farm

Smoothly

1."I can't catch mice," said the kit-ten on the farm. "I can't catch mice and my

tum-my feels hol-low." "Then my ad-vice," said the duck u-pon the pond, "then my ad-vice for a kit-ten to fol-low is to
(2.) my ad-vice," said the horse u-pon the hay, "then my ad-vice for a kit-ten to fol-low is to
(3.) my ad-vice," said the hen in-side the pen, "then my ad-vice for a kit-ten to fol-low is to
(4.) my ad-vice," said the cat u-pon the roof, "then my ad-vice for a kit-ten to fol-low is to

VERSES 1 TO 4 continue from here

quack quack quack out - side the far-mer's door, quack quack quack, then quack a lit-tle more, quack quack quack; the
neigh neigh neigh out - side the far-mer's door, neigh neigh neigh, then neigh a lit-tle more, neigh neigh neigh; the
cluck cluck cluck out - side the far-mer's door, cluck cluck cluck, then cluck a lit-tle more, cluck, cluck, cluck; the
miaow miaow miaow out - side the far-mer's door, miaow miaow miaow, then miaow a lit-tle more, miaow miaow miaow; the

VERSES 2, 3, 4 & 5 start here

B min   G   D/A   A7   D   A7

far-mer will be sure to find some bread for a kit-ten to swal-low." 2."But bread's not nice," said the kit-ten on the farm.
far-mer will be sure to find some oats for a kit-ten to swal-low." 3."But oats aren't nice," said the kit-ten on the farm.
far-mer will be sure to find some corn for a kit-ten to swal-low." 4."But corn's not nice," said the kit-ten on the farm.
far-mer will be sure to find some milk for a kit-ten to swal-low." 5."Now milk is nice," said the kit-ten on the farm.

D

Verse 2
A7

"Bread's not nice and my tum-my still feels hol-low." "Then
"Oats aren't nice and my
"Corn's not nice and my
"Milk is nice and my

Verse 3
A7

tum-my still feels oh so hol-low." "Then

Verse 4
A7

tum-my still feels oh so ter-rib-ly hol-low." "Then

Verse 5
A7

tum-my still feels oh so ter-rib-ly,

23

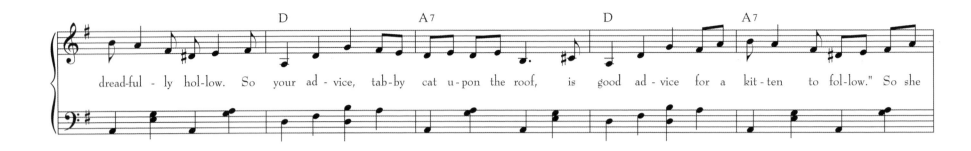

dread-ful - ly hol-low. So your ad-vice, tab-by cat u-pon the roof, is good ad-vice for a kit-ten to fol-low." So she

miaow miaow miaowed out-side the far-mer's door, miaow miaow miaowed then miaowed a lit-tle more, miaow miaow MIAOW, the

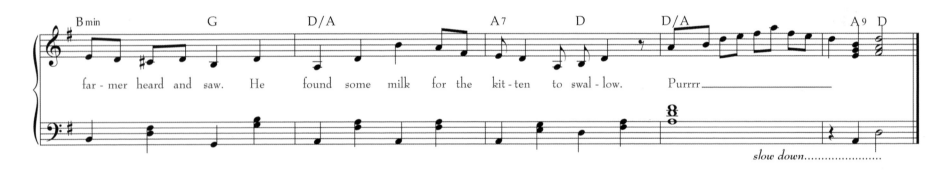

far-mer heard and saw. He found some milk for the kit-ten to swal-low. Purrrr_____

slow down......................

Verse 1

"I can't catch mice," said the kitten on the farm.
"I can't catch mice, and my tummy feels hollow."
"Then my advice," said the duck upon the pond,
"Then my advice for a kitten to follow
Is to *quack quack quack* outside the farmer's door,
Quack quack quack, then *quack* a little more,
Quack quack quack; the farmer will be sure
To find some bread for a kitten to swallow."

Verse 2

"But bread's not nice," said the kitten on the farm.
"Bread's not nice and my tummy still feels hollow."
"Then my advice," said the horse upon the hay,
"Then my advice for a kitten to follow
Is to *neigh neigh neigh* outside the farmer's door,
Neigh neigh neigh, then *neigh* a little more,
Neigh neigh neigh; the farmer will be sure
To find some oats for a kitten to swallow."

Verse 3

"But oats aren't nice," said the kitten on the farm.
"Oats aren't nice and my tummy still feels oh so hollow."
"Then my advice," said the hen inside the pen,
"Then my advice for a kitten to follow
Is to *cluck cluck cluck* outside the farmer's door,
Cluck cluck cluck, then *cluck* a little more,
Cluck cluck cluck; the farmer will be sure
To find some corn for a kitten to swallow."

Verse 4

"But corn's not nice," said the kitten on the farm.
"Corn's not nice and my tummy still feels oh so terribly hollow."
"Then my advice," said the cat upon the roof,
"Then my advice for a kitten to follow
Is to *miaow miaow miaow* outside the farmer's door,
Miaow miaow miaow, then *miaow* a little more,
Miaow miaow miaow; the farmer will be sure
To find some milk for a kitten to swallow."

Verse 5

"Now milk is nice," said the kitten on the farm.
"Milk is nice and my tummy still feels oh so terribly, dreadfully hollow.
So your advice, tabby cat upon the roof,
Is good advice for a kitten to follow."
So she *miaow miaow miaowed* outside the farmer's door,
Miaow miaow miaowed, then *miaowed* a little more,
Miaow miaow MIAOW, the farmer heard and saw.
He found some milk for the kitten to swallow. Purrrr.

The World Inside a Book

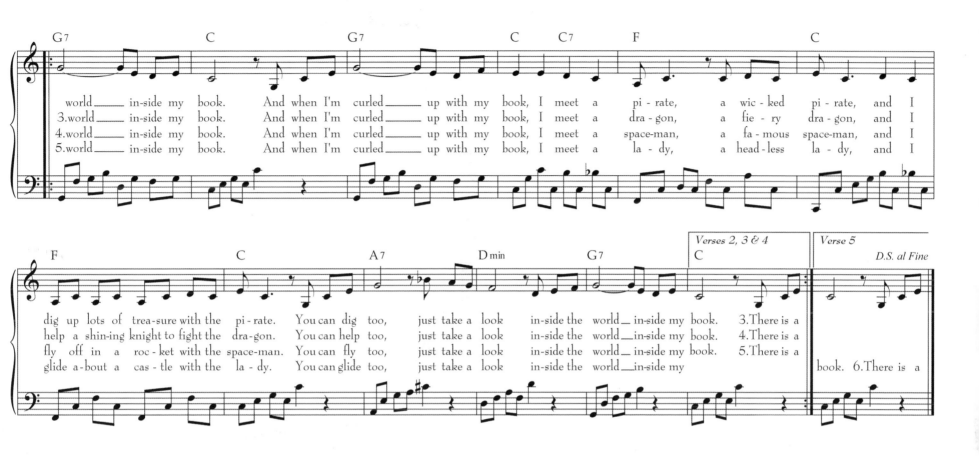

world____ in-side my book. And when I'm curled____ up with my book, I meet a pi - rate, a wic - ked pi - rate, and I
3. world____ in-side my book. And when I'm curled____ up with my book, I meet a dra - gon, a fie - ry dra - gon, and I
4. world____ in-side my book. And when I'm curled____ up with my book, I meet a space-man, a fa - mous space-man, and I
5. world____ in-side my book. And when I'm curled____ up with my book, I meet a la - dy, a head - less la - dy, and I

Verses 2, 3 & 4

Verse 5

D.S. al Fine

dig up lots of trea-sure with the pi - rate. You can dig too, just take a look in-side the world_ in-side my book. 3. There is a
help a shin-ing knight to fight the dra-gon. You can help too, just take a look in-side the world_in-side my book. 4. There is a
fly off in a roc - ket with the space-man. You can fly too, just take a look in-side the world_ in-side my book. 5. There is a
glide a-bout a cas - tle with the la - dy. You can glide too, just take a look in-side the world_in-side my book. 6. There is a

These lyrics are linked to CHARLIE COOK'S FAVOURITE BOOK, but you can also make up your own.

Verse 1

There is a world inside a book.
And when you're curled up with a book,
It doesn't matter what your age is,
You can take a flying leap into the pages.
So take a leap, and take a look
Inside the world inside a book.

Verse 2

There is a world inside my book.
And when I'm curled up with my book,
I meet a pirate, a wicked pirate,
And I dig up lots of treasure with the pirate.
You can dig too, just take a look
Inside the world inside my book.

Verse 3

There is a world inside my book.
And when I'm curled up with my book,
I meet a dragon, a fiery dragon,
And I help a shining knight to fight the dragon.
You can help too, just take a look
Inside the world inside my book.

Verse 4

There is a world inside my book.
And when I'm curled up with my book,
I meet a spaceman, a famous spaceman,
And I fly off in a rocket with the spaceman.
You can fly too, just take a look
Inside the world inside my book.

Verse 5

There is a world inside my book.
And when I'm curled up with my book,
I meet a lady, a headless lady,
And I glide about a castle with the lady.
You can glide too, just take a look
Inside the world inside my book.

Verse 6

There is a world inside a book.
And when you're curled up with a book,
It doesn't matter what your age is,
You can take a flying leap into the pages.
So take a leap, and take a look
Inside the world inside a book.

Swing and Spin

Swing tempo

We like to swing and spin.___ We like to swing and spin.___ We like to splish, splash, splosh. We like to

splish, splash, splosh. We like to jump like frogs. We like to jump like frogs, on and off logs, on and off logs. We like to

run, run, run, run, run in the sun.___ We like to run, run, run, run, run in the sun. And

dig, dig, dig, dig, dig in the sand. And dig, dig, dig, dig, dig in the sand. Stamp, stamp, stamp, stamp, stamp on the twigs.

Stamp, stamp, stamp, stamp, stamp on the twigs. And squ-elch, squ-elch, squelch in the mud. Squ-elch, squ-elch, squelch in the mud. We like to

We like to swing and spin.
We like to swing and spin.
We like to splish, splash, splosh.
We like to splish, splash, splosh.
We like to jump like frogs.
We like to jump like frogs,
On and off logs,
On and off logs.

We like to run, run, run, run, run in the sun.
We like to run, run, run, run, run in the sun.
And dig, dig, dig, dig, dig in the sand.
And dig, dig, dig, dig, dig in the sand.
Stamp, stamp, stamp, stamp, stamp, on the twigs.
Stamp, stamp, stamp, stamp, stamp, on the twigs.
And squelch, squelch, squelch in the mud.
Squelch, squelch, squelch in the mud.

skip, skip,skip. We like to skip, skip, skip. We like to hop, hop, hop. We like to hop, hop, hop. We like to tap, tap,tap. Let us in! Let us in!We like to

tap, tap, tap. Let us in! Let us in! And then, and then, we like to flop. We like to flop.

We like to skip, skip, skip.
We like to skip, skip, skip.
We like to hop, hop, hop.
We like to hop, hop, hop.
We like to tap, tap, tap. Let us in! Let us in!
We like to tap, tap, tap. Let us in! Let us in!

And then,
And then,
We like to flop.
We like to flop.

First published 2011 by Macmillan Children's Books
a division of Macmillan Publishers Limited
20 New Wharf Road, London N1 9RR
Basingstoke and Oxford
Associated companies throughout the world
www.panmacmillan.com

ISBN: 978-0-230-75875-9

A CIP catalogue record for this book is available from the British Library.

Printed in Belgium